any

D0606788

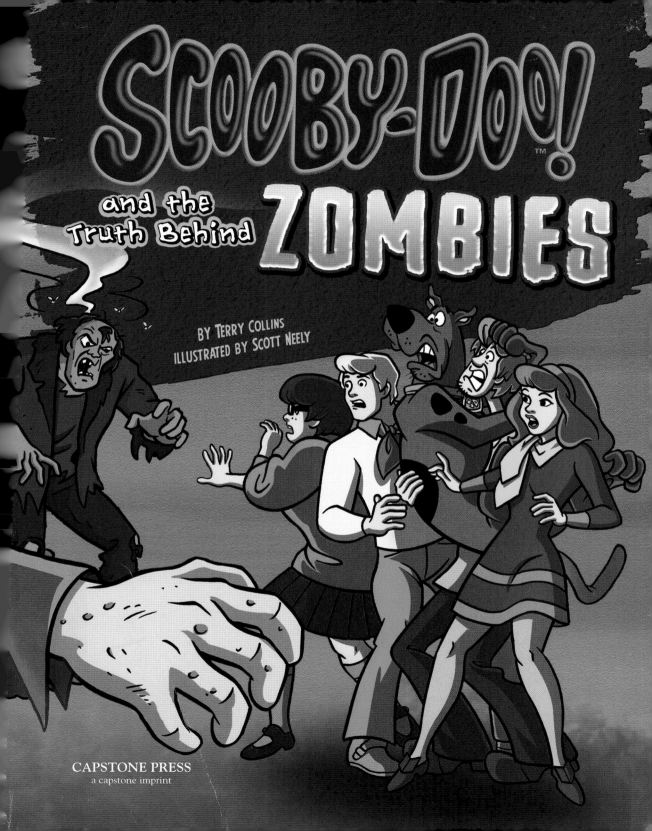

SCOOBY-DOO!

and the Truth Behind ZOMBIES

BY TERRY COLLINS

ILLUSTRATED BY SCOTT NEELY

CAPSTONE PRESS

a capstone imprint

Published in 2015 by Capstone Press,
A Capstone Imprint
1710 Roe Crest Drive
North Mankato, Minnesota 56003
www.capstonepub.com

Library of Congress Cataloging-in-Publication Data
Collins, Terry (Terry Lee), author.
Scooby-Doo! and the truth behind zombies /
by Terry Collins ; illustrated by Scott Neely.
pages cm. —— (Unmasking monsters with
Scooby-Doo!)
Summary: "The popular Scooby-Doo! and the Mystery
Inc. gang teach kids all about zombies"—— Provided
by publisher.
Audience: Ages 6–8.
Audience: K to grade 3.
Includes bibliographical references and index.
ISBN 978-1-4914-1796-6 (library binding)
1. Zombies——Juvenile literature. 2. Monsters——Juvenile
literature. 3. Curiosities and wonders——Juvenile literature.
I. Neely, Scott, illustrator. II. Title. III. Title: Zombies.
GR581.C65 2015
001.944——dc23   2014029123

Editorial Credits:
Editor: Shelly Lyons
Designer: Ted Williams
Art Director: Nathan Gassman
Production Specialist: Tori Abraham

Design Elements:
Shutterstock: ailin1, AllAnd, hugolacasse, Studiojumpee

The illustrations in this book were created traditionally,
with digital coloring.

Thanks to our adviser for her expertise, research,
and advice:
Elizabeth Tucker Gould, Professor of English
Binghamton University

Printed in the United States of America in
Stevens Point, Wisconsin
092014   008479WZS15

"Has anyone found Scooby yet?" Velma asked.

"The kitchen is all clear!" Shaggy replied.

"He wasn't in the Mystery Machine," said Fred.

"I found him!" said Daphne.

"Scooby-Doo!" Velma scolded. "Why are you hiding in the sofa?"

"Rombies!" yelled Scooby.

"Zombies are nothing to fear," said Daphne. "You just need to know more about them."

Well, voodoo zombies are quite different from other legendary zombies. In voodoo, a *bokor*, or sorcerer, makes people zombies.

A *bokor* gives his zombies a poisonous powder. The powder makes them his slaves.

"Are all zombies made by magic?" Shaggy asked.

"In movies and stories, zombies are created in other ways too," Velma replied. "Chemicals and even zombie viruses can turn people into zombies."

"So, always cover your nose when you sneeze, Scoob," Shaggy joked.

Velma smiled. "No sneezing necessary. But a zombie's bite can infect you, and then you become one of the walking dead!"

"Not that we're planning on looking ... ," Shaggy began.

"Uh-uh!" Scooby agreed, shaking his head.

"... but where can we find a zombie?" Shaggy finished.

"Wherever you want to look," said Fred. "According to legends environment doesn't affect zombies. They can live anywhere."

"Zoinks! That makes it even harder to hide!" Shaggy said.

"If hiding is no good, can I outrun a zombie?" Shaggy asked hopefully.

"Yes, you can," Velma said. "Running away from a zombie is always the best response in movies. But remember, even though zombies are slow, they never get tired."

"Luckily, as their bodies decay, they fall apart," Fred added. "Zombies are often missing a foot or a leg. Still, don't take them lightly."

Why? Are they stuck-up or something?
No, but often the only thing legendary zombies can say is "Uhhh, Uhhh." Their brains are mush, and some zombies have no tongues.
YUCK!

"Well, stories say that zombies eat fresh meat from any living creature," Daphne continued. "Birds, horses ... dogs."

"Ruh, roh!" Scooby exclaimed.

"And um, people," Fred finished. "Some zombies' favorite thing to eat is human brains."

Please don't feed the Zombies.

Why not? Ol' Frankie looks like a zombie to me!
Frankenstein was sewn together with body parts from many dead people, not just one. Also, the monster can think, learns to talk, and he doesn't want to eat your brain.

They have no powers, unless you include being super-stinky.
P-U!
A zombie smells like rotting flesh.

How can we protect ourselves against legendary zombies?
REAH!
Always carry something that makes a loud noise. Throw it away from you. Zombies will follow the sound, letting you escape.
RINGGG!

You should also always protect your body. Wear leather boots that cover your legs and feet.

Thick leather gloves keep hands and fingers safe. Layers of clothing help to avoid a zombie's bite. Also, never travel alone around zombies!

"Don't worry," Shaggy said. "With all of this great information, we can handle any old zombie that crosses our path! Right, Scoob?"

"It looks like Shaggy and Scooby found a great hiding spot!" said Daphne.

"Well, Scooby and Shaggy always were fast learners," laughed Velma.

GLOSSARY

chemical—a substance that creates a reaction

decay—to break down into tiny pieces after dying

flesh—the soft part of an animal's body that covers the bones

infect—to cause disease by introducing germs or viruses

legend—a story handed down from earlier times; it is often based on fact, but it is not entirely true

virus—a germ that infects living things and causes disease

READ MORE

O'Hearn, Michael. *Zombies vs. Mummies: Clash of the Living Dead.* Mankato, Minn.: Capstone Press, 2012.

Troupe, Thomas Kingsley. *The Legend of the Zombie.* Legend Has It. Mankato, Minn.: Picture Window Books, 2012.

INTERNET SITES

FactHound offers a safe, fun way to find Internet sites related to this book. All of the sites on FactHound have been researched by our staff.

Here's all you do:

Visit *www.facthound.com*

Type in this code: 9781491417966

Super-cool stuff! Check out projects, games and lots more at **www.capstonekids.com**

INDEX